#Poverty_to_6_figures ~ Break th

MW01493403

Published by Rachel L. Gary

Copyright ©2025 by Rachel L. Gary

Paper Back ISBN 978-2-8972-7135-0

I dedicate this book to my loves that make all of this worthwhile.

To my continues Tre and Jae I am proud of the people you are and to the developing adults you are becoming. Being your mother, I have found that impossible can't and will not be an option because of you I'mPossible.

To my wife Marie, your tolerance of all the long days and nights waiting up patiently as I burned both ends of a very short candle forced me to develop my 4-S strategy. I love the patience that you have taught me to have with myself, that has made me a better partner, parent, follower, and leader.

To my bonus sons Kenny and Dentral I am so grateful for the opportunity to be your other parent. The discussions about life and the challenges within it reminded me that giving to new leaders was my responsibility. I see you both as the leaders you are, keep moving the needle in others lives.

Introduction: Rising from the Ashes

"Impossible does not exist; the word itself says I'mPossible." - Rachel L.Gary

---

When I look back, it's clear, my story isn't just about surviving, it's about rising from the ashes, burning through every obstacle thrown my way. From *Forged In Fire*, you saw the beginnings, the trials, the losses, the confusion. But this chapter? This is where things get real.

I went from being that girl trying to figure out how to get by, literally just trying to find a way to eat to building a life most only dream of. I started with nothing: no resources, no education, no guidance. But I didn't stop there. I didn't just learn how to eat; I figured out how to bring home the bacon consistently. And then, I took that bacon and turned it into a feast.

This isn't a quick-fix, get-rich story. This is the real, unfiltered journey of a Black girl in America who rose out of poverty, who defied the odds, and made it happen. Every hurdle I faced wasn't just something to get over, it was a catalyst, propelling me to the next level.

You're going to see the transformation, the shift from a mindset of scarcity to one of abundance. You'll witness the habits, the action plans, the mentors, and the techniques that took me from scraping by to achieving multiple six-figure success.

My circumstances didn't define me; they became the fire that lit the way. And if I can do it, so can you. This journey is proof that where you start has nothing to do with where you can go.

So let's begin. This is your blueprint to develop the greatness in you.

Chapter 1: The First Spark - Preparing for Promotion

I couldn't believe it when I was offered the promotion. It felt surreal, like I was living someone else's life. Three months into my new role, and here I was, already being noticed. My mind flashed back to where I was just one year ago, across the street on the manufacturing line, earning $6.75 an hour, busting my back in a job that made me feel as if I was losing my grip on reality. I'd go home every day, not to my own place, but to someone else's house. My kids and I were welcome there, but we weren't home. We slept on an air mattress, the kind you have to re-inflate every night because it slowly leaks air, like my life had been leaking hope.

I remember that January like it was yesterday. It was a cold 20 degrees night in Chicago, and I was sitting outside on the front porch, freezing. There was something about that cold, about being uncomfortable, that woke something up in me. I had a notebook in my hand, and I started writing. I wrote down everything I wanted out of life, no matter how far-fetched it seemed at the time. I closed my eyes, thought hard about who I needed to *be* to get what I wanted, and I wrote that down, too. I envisioned a version of myself I hadn't met yet, the one who wasn't just surviving but thriving.

Then, I did something that changed everything. I wrote down how I had gotten here, right to this cold front porch, to the air mattress, to this job that I liked but was never going to pay enough. I listed every bad decision, every missed opportunity, every habit that was holding me back. This wasn't a pity party, far from it. I knew that if I didn't figure out exactly how I had gotten here, I'd be right back in the same place, on that same air mattress, and I wasn't having it. Not anymore.

That night, I asked myself the hard questions, the ones I'd been avoiding for so long.

- *What from my past am I holding on to?*
- *What limiting beliefs am I still clinging to?*
- *What decisions or actions led me to this exact moment?*
- *What patterns or habits do I keep repeating that are sabotaging me?*
- *What have I been avoiding or neglecting that's contributed to this outcome?*

I dug deep, facing the parts of me that I had kept buried. It wasn't easy, but it was necessary. I had to get real with myself. No more blaming the world, no more excuses. If I wanted to get out of this, if I wanted to be more than just a bystander in my own life, I had to take ownership.

After answering those hard questions, it became crystal clear that I needed to make some changes. But not the superficial kind, the deep, uncomfortable ones. The kind that doesn't just rearrange your life but rearrange who you are.

One of the biggest realizations I had was that I had spent too much time living other people's lives. I was too wrapped up in what other people were doing, too concerned with their opinions, their successes, their failures, and I wasn't paying attention to my own life. I had become a bystander, watching myself from the outside, disconnected from my own dreams. That had to stop.

I knew I had to start loving myself first. I had to understand that the version of me I wanted to become couldn't exist without radical self-love and self-respect. Loving myself meant setting boundaries, hard ones. I wasn't going to let myself off the hook anymore. I wasn't going to let fear or doubt creep in and dictate my choices. I needed to be clear on what I wanted and spend time with those wants every single day.

I made a commitment to myself:

- Every day, I'd set one small goal that I would complete by 8 p.m., no excuses.
- I'd go to the library and pick up a book related to my goals, read it by the end of the week, and then implement what I learned in the following week.
- I'd stay focused on my *"Y"*, that deeper reason driving me to change my life.

As someone who has always been a voracious reader, I knew that knowledge was power. I dove into books like my life depended on it because, in a way, it did. If I didn't start filling my mind with the right kind of knowledge, I'd be stuck forever, repeating the same mistakes, running in circles.

It was all about consistency. Every day, I would take one small step forward, no matter how insignificant it seemed at the time. Those small steps added up. They started to create momentum, and with each new action, I felt myself getting closer to my goals. I wasn't just surviving anymore, I was starting to thrive. The version of myself I had written about on that cold January night was slowly becoming a reality.

The truth is, none of this would have been possible without the techniques that eventually became the foundation of my *B.E.G.I.N.* course. I built my life on what I now call the "4-S Pillars of Self," and these principles were essential in transforming me from someone barely surviving to someone thriving and building a life of abundance. These pillars shaped my mindset, my habits, and ultimately, my success.

The 4 Pillars of Self are:

1. **Self-Esteem:** Before I could begin my journey, I had to believe I was worthy of the life I dreamed of. I needed to reclaim my sense of self-worth, to understand that I wasn't defined by my

past mistakes or current circumstances. I had to see myself as deserving of success, happiness, and abundance. This shift in how I viewed myself was crucial. Without self-esteem, I wouldn't have had the courage to pursue opportunities or the resilience to keep going when things got tough.

2. **Self-Discipline:** This was the cornerstone of my transformation. It wasn't enough to simply want a better life, I had to commit to the daily actions that would get me there. Self-discipline meant stepping up for myself, sticking to my goals, and following through, even on days when I didn't feel like it. It was the difference between wishing for success and working for it. Every day I had to show up, do the work, and hold myself accountable.

3. **Self-Care:** Along the way, I realized that I couldn't pour from an empty cup. Self-care wasn't about luxury; it was about necessity. I needed to take care of my mind, body, and spirit so I could be strong enough to keep pushing forward. This meant establishing routines that allowed me to recharge, setting healthy boundaries with others, and carving out time for myself. Self-care helped me stay balanced, focused, and energized for the journey ahead.

4. **Self-Awareness:** I had to face my truth before I could change my life. Self-awareness was about looking at myself, honestly and without judgment, and recognizing the patterns, habits, and beliefs that were holding me back. I had to identify my blind spots and take ownership of my past decisions. This self-awareness allowed me to make conscious choices and avoid falling back into old habits that no longer served me.

These four pillars became my foundation. They weren't just strategies or concepts, they were a new way of living. They transformed the way I thought, the way I acted, and the way I moved towards my goals. They are what helped me rise from that air mattress to the moment I was preparing for my first promotion.

That promotion wasn't just a milestone; it was proof that the habits and techniques I had built were working. It was the first tangible result of the inner work I had done and the spark that ignited the journey from poverty_to_six_figures. With self-esteem, self-discipline, self-care, and self-awareness, I had equipped myself with the tools I needed to not just survive, but to create a life I once only dreamed about.

This is where the real journey began. That promotion opened the door to the possibilities I had only written about in my notebook on that freezing January night. It was the first step on a path that would lead me to financial freedom, personal fulfillment, and the ability to help others walk the same path. The techniques I had built in those early days are the same ones I teach within the **Say I'mPossible Academy** inside the **B.E.G.I.N.** course, because they are the foundation for lasting success. And it all started with that first spark.

FIGURE 1.1 Your Turn: *"You are the C.E.O. Action Plan"*

Alright, this is the part where the rubber meets the road. I'm all about action, because knowing is one thing, but doing is what creates real change. Now,it's time to introduce you to the C.E.O. of your life which means having **Clarity in your actions, being Empowered by your choices, and Owning your direction**. That's what I want you to live by as you move through this book, and beyond.

Each chapter will end with a *"You are the C.E.O. Action Plan"* because I want you to not just *read* this book, but to actively *work* through it. By the time you finish, I want you to *own* the fact that you are the C.E.O. of your life. No more waiting, wishing, or hoping for someone to hand you a promotion, a break, or an opportunity. It's time for you to create your own.

Let's start by working through the **4 Pillars of Self** that I laid out in this chapter. These pillars will be the foundation of your journey, just like they were for me.

1. Self-Esteem:

- **Clarity:** Get clear about how you see yourself. What story are you telling yourself about who you are and what you deserve?
- **Empowerment:** Challenge the negative beliefs you've been holding on to. For every "I can't" or "I'm not good enough," replace it with "I can" and "I am worthy."
- **Ownership:** Write down one thing you believe you deserve in life, whether it's a promotion, financial stability, or personal peace, and affirm that it's yours to claim.

2. Self-Discipline:

- **Clarity:** Identify one small, manageable goal that aligns with your bigger Why. What action can you take today that moves you toward that goal?

9

- **Empowerment:** Commit to doing this one thing every day for the next seven days. Just one. By completing this, you're proving to yourself that you can stay disciplined, even when the going gets tough.
- **Ownership:** Track your progress. Own your wins, no matter how small they seem. Success is built one step at a time, and every step matters.

3. Self-Care:

- **Clarity:** Recognize where you've been neglecting yourself. What areas of your life need more attention, your mental, physical, or emotional health?
- **Empowerment:** Choose one self-care practice to add to your daily routine. It could be as simple as taking a 10-minute break to breathe, stretch, or reflect. This isn't a luxury, it's a necessity for your success.
- **Ownership:** Set boundaries. What distractions or obligations are stealing your energy? Decide what you need to say "no" to, so you can say "yes" to yourself.

4. Self-Awareness:

- **Clarity:** Take an honest look at your habits. What patterns are holding you back? Where are you repeating the same mistakes?
- **Empowerment:** Make a conscious decision to break one negative habit this week. Whether it's procrastination, self-doubt, or fear of failure, commit to making a shift.
- **Ownership:** Reflect on your journey so far. What have you learned about yourself? Own that growth and celebrate the progress you're making, even if it feels small.

Action Step:

Write down these questions and work through them. Hold yourself accountable. Remember, being the C.E.O. isn't just a title, it's a mindset, a way of living. It's about taking charge of your actions, your decisions, and your future.

Bonus:

I want you to create your own C.E.O. statement. Here's a prompt to get you started:

"As the C.E.O. of my life, I will take control of _____ by _____."

Fill in the blanks with something specific. Ensure that you put the exact date and time for specificity. It could be a behavior you want to change, a habit you want to form, or a goal you're ready to pursue. Keep this statement with you as you move through the rest of the book.

Remember: you are not a bystander in your own life anymore. You are the C.E.O., and it's time to start acting like it. Let's go!

Chapter 2: Building the Foundation

One of the most important things I've learned is that **intentionality** can make or break the life you're trying to build. It's not enough to want something, you have to be crystal clear about **"Y"** you want it and how you're going to get there. For me, that clarity came when I asked myself the most pivotal question: *Why am I doing this?* My answer was simple but powerful: I wanted to become someone my kids could be proud of! That desire became my driving force, my North Star, and ultimately the foundation of the plan that would change my life.

But a goal without a plan is just a dream. And I didn't have time for wishful thinking, I had to put action behind my intentions. To do that, I needed a framework, something concrete that would take my big goal and break it down into something achievable.

After doing my research, I found the **S.M.A.R.T. goal framework**, and that was when things started to shift. S.M.A.R.T. stands for Specific, Measurable, Achievable, Relevant, and Time-Based, and it was exactly the structure I needed to turn my vision into a step-by-step plan.

Before I could even start setting my goals, I had to get clear on my **"Why."** This wasn't some surface-level reason; it was something deep. Something that pulled at my heart every day. I wanted to become the person my children could look up to. That was it. It wasn't about the money, the title, or the accolades. It was about **pride**, not just my pride in myself, but my kids' pride in who I was becoming.

To be honest, that **"Y"** kept me grounded when everything else felt chaotic. The long work hours, the overwhelming exhaustion, the obstacles that seemed to spring up at every turn, my **"Y"** was the fuel that kept me going.

And here's why this matters: **Your "Y" has to be so powerful that it anchors you.** It has to pull you through the rough days when you're running on empty and your goals feel impossibly far away. Once you establish your "Y," every action you take will be a reflection of that purpose. It becomes the lens through which you see everything.

After I got clear on my "Y," I realized that wanting to become someone my kids could be proud of wasn't enough on its own. I needed to **break it down** into actionable steps. That's where S.M.A.R.T. came into play. It gave me the structure to turn my vision into a series of goals I could measure, track, and accomplish.

Here's how it works and how I applied it:

1. **Specific: The goal needed to be clear, not some vague idea about "becoming better."** I got specific about what I wanted. My focus wasn't just to *be* someone my kids would be proud of; it was to become a leader both in my personal life and professional career. I wanted to climb out of the situation I was in and create a life where my kids saw me as a role model, a leader who takes charge of her life.
2. **Measurable: How would I know if I was on track?** I knew that I couldn't just base my success on feelings. I needed hard facts, milestones that would let me measure my progress. For me, that meant tracking things like my shift of career promotions, the money I was able to save or invest, and, eventually, the feedback I was getting from my kids. It also meant taking note of smaller wins: Am I more present? Am I more patient? Am I setting a better example each day?
3. **Achievable: I wasn't setting myself up for failure by setting goals that were too far out of reach.** This isn't to say I didn't aim high, but I aimed **strategically**. I focused on making real progress, step by step. For example, I knew I couldn't go from my current job straight into an executive role overnight, but I

could work toward promotions within my organization, gaining more responsibility and influence as I went.

4. **Relevant: Every goal had to align with my larger purpose.** Becoming a better mother, role model, and leader wasn't just about climbing the career ladder, it was about ensuring that every goal I set was **in service of my bigger picture.** If something didn't line up with my "Why," it wasn't worth my time. That meant I had to get serious about cutting out distractions and focusing only on what would move me closer to my vision.

5. **Time-Based: Setting deadlines was crucial.** Without a timeline, goals become slippery, easy to push off until tomorrow or next week or next month. I had to hold myself accountable. That meant giving myself hard deadlines. "In two months we will have our own place, In three months, I'll apply for a promotion." "By the end of the year, I'll have saved X amount of money." Deadlines kept me moving forward, especially on days when it would have been easier to coast.

Once I had established my **"Y"** and applied the S.M.A.R.T. framework, I began breaking that big goal down into **mindsets, behaviors, and activities.**

Let's talk about **mindsets** first. In order to become the person I envisioned, I had to shift my thinking. Success wasn't just going to happen to me, I had to build it. I needed to cultivate a mindset of **growth** and **resilience**. I knew that self-doubt would creep in (and it did), but I committed to **believing** that I was worthy of the success I was striving for. That's the first mindset shift: moving from doubt to belief. Using positive affirmations daily as I grew kept me centered.

Next, I had to focus on my **behaviors.** I started observing people who were where I wanted to be. What did they do differently? How did they carry themselves? How did they make decisions? I started to model my actions after theirs. I learned that successful people have consistent, intentional behaviors, they don't leave things to chance. They plan, they prepare, and they execute.

Finally, there were the **activities**. I knew that achieving my goals would require me to take tangible steps every day. I started scheduling time for **personal development**, reading books, listening to motivational speeches, setting aside time to journal, and reflect on my progress. I had to actively engage in my own growth, not just passively hope that things would change.

One thing I learned early on was the importance of **tracking progress**. When you set goals, it's easy to get lost in the day-to-day grind and forget how far you've come. That's why I made a point of **writing things down**.

Every month, I would sit down and reflect on my progress. What worked? What didn't? Where did I fall short, and where did I excel? This wasn't about beating myself up over missed opportunities, it was about **learning** from them and adjusting my strategy.

By keeping a record of my progress, I was able to **stay motivated**. Even when it felt like I wasn't moving fast enough, I could look back and see just how far I had come. Celebrate those small wins because they mattered, they added up to something bigger over time.

At the end of the day, goal setting isn't just about checking boxes on a to-do list. It's about **becoming** the person you need to be in order to achieve the life you desire. You can't just set goals and hope they magically happen. You have to **own** every step of the process, be intentional about your "Why," use a framework like S.M.A.R.T., and be willing to put in the work day after day.

Remember: **You are the CEO of your life.** Every decision, every action, and every goal you set moves you closer to the person you're destined to become. Stay focused, stay driven, and most importantly, stay true to your "Y." That's how you create lasting change.

When you're trying to move toward success, it's not just about setting big goals, it's about the **habits** you build to sustain that journey. And for me, the first habit I had to cultivate wasn't about time management or productivity. It was about reshaping my **mindset**.

You see, for years, I carried the weight of my past like an anchor. The doubts, the failures, the moments where I didn't feel good enough, they followed me everywhere, even into my dreams. I spent so much time wanting to be accepted, loved, and respected by others, but in doing so, I forgot the most important person in my life: **me**.

It took time to realize that if I wanted to be truly successful, I had to let go of those old narratives. I had to stop reliving the past and accept that I wasn't perfect, but I was capable of **growing** from it. That was my first step toward real transformation, learning to **respect** myself, my time, my energy, and most importantly, my **strengths**.

The process of letting go of negative thoughts didn't happen overnight. It was hard. But here's the thing about success: it's often rooted in **mental discipline** before anything else. If I wanted to build a successful life, I had to start by building a successful **mindset**.

So, I made a commitment to myself to actively **replace negativity** with positivity. Every day, I made it a point to feed my mind with motivational words and uplifting stories. I turned to leaders like **Les Brown** and **Zig Ziglar**, two people whose words helped me see that I was worthy of the life I wanted. Twice a day, for a total of two hours, I listened to them speak about the power of belief, resilience, and the relentless pursuit of your dreams.

I kept that routine going for two months straight. Every morning and every evening, I let their words fill my mind, slowly replacing the doubt that had taken root there for so many years. Their voices became part of my daily routine, my **well of positivity** that I could draw from whenever I felt the old doubts creeping back in.

And it worked. Over time, my belief in myself grew stronger. I started to believe that I was worthy of success, that I was capable of achieving my goals, and that my past didn't define me. As I stated in **part 1 of the E.P.I.C. Collection, Forged in Fire**. "You are not defined by the challenges you face, but by how you rise to meet them." That belief was the foundation for everything that came next.

It wasn't just about listening to motivational speakers, though. I knew that if I wanted to change my life, I had to start by building myself up from the inside out. That's where the **Pillars of Self** came in.

For me, the first two pillars, **Self-Esteem** and **Self-Care**, were critical in developing the habits that would drive my success. These pillars helped me realize that if I didn't take care of myself, both physically and mentally, I wouldn't have the strength to push forward.

- **Self-Esteem** meant recognizing my own worth. It meant knowing that I had value, even when the world around me seemed to suggest otherwise. I had to remind myself every day that I was deserving of the goals I was pursuing. That wasn't easy, but I kept at it. I used daily affirmations to reinforce that belief: *I am strong. I am capable. I am deserving of success.*
- **Self-Care** wasn't just about treating myself to rest or relaxation (although that's important too). It was about **respecting my time** and energy. I had to stop giving away so much of myself to things or people that didn't serve my bigger goals. This meant creating **boundaries**, saying "no" to distractions and staying focused on what really mattered.

These two pillars gave me the **mental and emotional resilience** I needed to keep moving forward, even on the hard days.

When it comes to building habits that foster success, **discipline** is the secret sauce. Without it, even the best intentions can fall apart. And trust me, I wasn't always the most disciplined person. But once I set my mind on becoming someone my kids could be proud of, my discipline became **unwavering**.

Let me give you an example: At one point, I was working 12-hour days and traveling an hour each way by bus. My schedule was grueling, and it would have been so easy to let my goals slip through the cracks. But I didn't. Instead, I made a habit of reviewing my **daily goals,** every single day.

No matter how tired I was, I would take time each night to **evaluate** my progress and **reevaluate** my plans. Did I hit my goals for the day? If not, why? What adjustments did I need to make? This constant cycle of setting, evaluating, and adjusting my goals became a core part of my daily routine. It was my way of holding myself accountable and ensuring that I was always moving forward, even if it was just by an inch at a time.

At the end of the day, all of these habits, replacing negative thoughts, building self-esteem and self-care, and maintaining self-discipline, were rooted in a bigger purpose. It wasn't just about checking off boxes on a to-do list. It was about **becoming the person I was meant to be**, the person my kids could look up to.

That purpose is what kept me going, day after day. It's what pushed me to listen to motivational speakers when I was tired, to reflect on my goals when I was worn out from a long day of work, and to keep believing in myself even when it would have been easier to quit.

What I've learned from this journey is that habits aren't just about the actions you take. They're about the **mindset** you cultivate. It's easy to fall into the trap of thinking that success is just about doing more, more work, more effort, more hustle. But it's not. Success is about **consistency**. It's about living in **integrity** doing the right things, day in and day out, even when it's hard. Even when no one else is watching.

For me, that meant sticking to my daily routine, no matter how busy I was. It meant holding myself accountable, setting and resetting my goals, and staying grounded in my purpose. It meant believing in myself when others didn't.

At the end of the day, the habits you build today will shape the future you walk into tomorrow. If there's one thing I've learned, it's this: **Your habits determine your future**. If you want success, you have to be willing to put in the work, day after day, without shortcuts.

So, start small if you have to. Build one habit, then another, and then another. And before you know it, you'll look back and realize just how far those small, daily steps have taken you. **That's the power of habits.**

Every day is filled with decisions, and those choices either push us forward or pull us back. For me, empowerment meant **making decisions** that aligned with my long-term goals and the life I wanted for myself and my family. It wasn't about just doing enough to get by, it was about being **intentional** in every part of my life, no matter how small the decision seemed.

I made a commitment to immerse myself in positivity. The only music I listened to was motivational, songs that filled my spirit and reminded me of my potential. The same went for TV, I wasn't interested in watching anything that didn't feed my **growth**. I had no time for negativity because I was dedicated to my evolution. I wasn't just showing up at work anymore; I was showing up to be the **best version** of myself.

At work, this looked like collaboration, celebration, and always lending a hand. I realized early on that true leadership isn't about being the loudest or most visible person in the room. It's about contributing to the success of those around you. I kept my energy **positive**, avoided complaining, and became a person who offered **solutions** instead of excuses. This not only built my reputation but also aligned with my long-term vision of becoming someone my kids could look up to, a person of **integrity** and action.

But empowerment didn't stop at work. At home, it was just as important to make choices that would help my children grow into **intelligent**, respectful individuals. I taught them that our circumstances didn't define us, but our **choices** did. I wanted them to understand that **knowledge is power**, and so we spent time reading books that would give them the wisdom of the past. I didn't just want them to follow instructions blindly; I wanted them to think for themselves, to question the world around them, and to understand the consequences of their actions.

I made sure they knew that respect was not just something they were owed, but something they needed to **give** as well. Where we lived, the environment didn't dictate our worth. We didn't let the limitations of our surroundings define us. The ghetto stopped at our door because we carried ourselves with pride, purpose, and intelligence. **We knew who we were**, and we knew where we were going.

Empowerment through choices isn't just a nice idea; it's a daily practice. It's about making decisions that are aligned with the future you want, no matter how hard or inconvenient they may seem at the moment. Every choice, every action, every habit adds up over time, and when you're intentional, those decisions create a life that's not only successful but **fulfilling**.

Figure 2.1 It's Your Turn: You're the C.E.O. Action Plan, Building the Foundation

You've made it this far, and now it's time to take action. I'm not just here to share stories; I'm here to guide you toward becoming the **C.E.O. of your life**. Remember, being a C.E.O. isn't just a title, it's a mindset. C.E.O. stands for **Clarity** in your actions, **Empowered** by your choices, and **Owning** your direction.

This plan isn't about someday or maybe. It's about **today** and taking real, actionable steps to build the life you deserve. By the end of this book, I want you to **own** that you are the C.E.O. of your life, and that means it's time to start now.

1. Establishing Your "Y": Creating Clarity

Your first task as the C.E.O. is to get **crystal clear** on your goals. It's not enough to want something, you need to define it in detail. The **"Y"** behind your goal is your **north star**, guiding every step you take. Whether it's becoming someone your kids are proud of or achieving financial independence, **write it down**.

Here's what you need to do:

- **Define Your Why:** Why are you chasing this goal? What does it mean to you?_____

_____

2. Developing Habits: Daily Routines and Habits That Foster Success

Now that you have your "Y" you're set, it's time to build the habits that will make them a reality. Success isn't built on what we do once in a while, it's built on what we do **daily**. To become the person who achieves those goals, you need to be **intentional** with your time, energy, and mindset.

Here's how you can get started:

- **Start Small:** Identify **one daily habit** you can implement right away. It could be as simple as journaling for 10 minutes or reading a chapter of a book that aligns with your goals.
- **Feed Your Mind Positivity:** Dive into motivational content like I did with Les Brown and Zig Ziglar. Fill your mind with positivity **twice a day**, morning, and night to set your tone for success.
- **Reflect Daily:** At the end of each day, ask yourself, "Did I make progress toward my Why today?" If not, why? Adjust your habits and routines until they align with your goals.

Self-discipline and consistency will turn small habits into **big results**. Every step forward matters, and with each day, you'll get closer to where you want to be.

Embracing the C.E.O. Mindset

Here's what I need you to understand: **Impossible isn't a part of our vocabulary**. The word itself says "I'mPossible." You are capable of achieving more than you've ever imagined. If you **own** I'mPossible. Go to https://nfjj0f-0w.myshopify.com/ Put in code **"#CEOMindset" to get 50% of your I'mPossible swag.**

Each day, you will build clarity, feel empowered by your choices, and take full ownership of the direction you're going. By following this plan, you're laying the foundation for the life you've always wanted. **You're in control**, never forget that.

Write Your Affirmations:

Affirmations are powerful tools to help you stay focused on your goals and remind you of your strength. Now that you've established your Why and started building your habits, it's time to solidify your belief in yourself.

Here are two spaces for your affirmations. Take a moment and write two affirmations that will inspire you to keep moving forward:

Affirmation 1:
(Example: "I am the architect of my life, and each step I take brings me closer to my vision.")

Affirmation 2:
(Example: "Every decision I make today is setting the foundation for my future success.")

Direction:

- Make sure these affirmations resonate with your "Y".
- Repeat them daily, especially in the moments when doubt creeps in.
- Affirmations should feel **personal** and **empowering**, they're your verbal commitment to yourself.

Remember, you are the **C.E.O. of your life,** and every action you take matters. **Let's get to work!**

Chapter 3: Conquering Fear

Fear. It's a part of life, something we all experience, but for many, fear can feel like an immovable barrier between where you are and where you want to be. The truth is, fear isn't always a reflection of reality; it's a conditioned response designed to protect us, but more often than not, it holds us back. As Lisa Nichols motivational speaker and author of Abundance Now puts it, **"F.E.A.R. is F.ake E.vidence A.ppearing R.eal."** It's your mind's way of trying to convince you to stay within the familiar, the safe zone. But here's the thing: **growth doesn't happen in the safe zone.**

If you're reading this, it means you're ready to move past that fear and step into your potential as the **C.E.O. of your life.** And as a C.E.O., you're expected to show **Clarity** in your actions, be **Empowered** by your choices, and take **Ownership** of your direction. Fear may try to convince you that stepping into the unknown is dangerous, but what's truly dangerous is letting fear make the decisions for you.

Let's start by recognizing that fear, especially when you're trying to grow, is normal. It's something we all experience, but the difference between success and staying stuck is how you respond to it. We were conditioned from a young age to associate fear with anything that goes outside the boundaries of what's familiar. From birth to the age of three, we're told **no** and **stop** thousands of times. Think about that! This is during the time when we're most curious and eager to learn about the world, but out of love, our parents often stifle that curiosity, trying to protect us from harm.

As we get older, this conditioning continues. Teachers, authority figures, even our peers reinforce this idea that staying within the lines is safer. "Follow the leader," "don't run," "sit down," "be quiet", all of these commands are meant to keep us controlled, but they also teach us to be afraid of stepping out of the box. The fear of making mistakes, being judged, or failing is rooted in these early experiences, and unless we confront them, they'll continue to control us.

Now, as an adult, you might not even realize how deep these fears run. You might be afraid of failure, of rejection, of making the wrong decision. But ask yourself this: **What's scarier, the fear itself or the regret of not trying?** Fear may seem real in the moment, but when you break it down, it's just a story you've been telling yourself. The good news is you can change that story.

To confront fear, you first need to identify it. Ask yourself: What exactly am I afraid of? Name it. Be specific. Once you identify the fear, you can start to understand where it's coming from and why it's showing up. Is it fear of failure? Fear of being judged? Fear of success? Sometimes, the fear of actually getting what you want can be just as powerful as the fear of not getting it.

So now that we've identified the fear, let's talk about how to overcome it. Fear is like an overprotective friend, it means well, but it doesn't always know what's best for you. Your job as the **C.E.O. of your life** is to acknowledge fear, thank it for its concern, but ultimately keep moving forward. Here's how:

1. **Challenge Your Thoughts**: Fear often lives in the mind as a "what if." What if I fail? What if I embarrass myself? What if I'm not good enough? These thoughts are just that, thoughts. They're not facts. When fear starts speaking, challenge it. Ask yourself, "Is this really true? Or am I imagining the worst-case scenario?" More often than not, you'll find that fear exaggerates the risk and minimizes your ability to succeed.
2. **Take Action, Even If It's Small**: Fear wants you to stay frozen in place, but the only way to combat it is through action. Start small if you have to, but do something. When I first started to confront my own fears, I realized that the scariest part was not

the action itself, but the anticipation. Once you take that first step, you'll often find that the fear starts to lose its grip. Success comes from momentum, and every small action builds that momentum.

3. **Reframe Failure**: One of the biggest fears that holds people back is the fear of failure. But here's the thing, failure is not the end. It's part of the process. Every time you fail, you're learning something valuable. You're gathering data on what works and what doesn't, and that's crucial to your growth. Reframe failure not as a setback, but as a stepping stone. The most successful people in the world have failed more times than they've succeeded. It's not about avoiding failure; it's about **failing forward**.

4. **Surround Yourself with Positivity**: Fear feeds on negativity, so you need to make sure you're surrounding yourself with the right people and the right environment. Limit your exposure to negativity, whether it's people who constantly doubt you or media that fills you with anxiety. Instead, fill your mind with positivity. Motivational speeches, uplifting books, mentors who push you to be better, these are the tools that will help you stay focused and push through fear.

5. **Visualize Your Success**: When fear sets in, your mind tends to focus on the worst-case scenario. But you have the power to shift that focus. Instead of dwelling on what could go wrong, visualize everything going right. Imagine yourself achieving your goals, overcoming obstacles, and succeeding. When you start to focus on the positive, your mind shifts from fear to possibility.

Let me share a story from my own life that really illustrates how I had to confront my fears head-on.

When I took that first leadership role I was afraid. On paper, it seemed like the next logical step, but internally, I was terrified. I was afraid of failing, afraid of not being respected, and afraid of letting down the people who believed in me. That fear was so strong that for a moment, I considered turning down the offer just to avoid the possibility of failing.

But I had to remind myself: **What's the worst that could happen?** Yes, I could fail. But what if I didn't? What if I thrived in this role? The only way to know was to try. So I did. I took the role, and guess what? It wasn't easy. There were challenges, setbacks, and yes, even some failures along the way. But every time I pushed through a fear, I came out stronger, more confident, and more capable.

In the end, that leadership role wasn't just about advancing in my career; it was about proving to myself that fear didn't get to make the decisions. I did. And that's the power you hold too.

Fear is a natural part of the journey, but it doesn't have to be the thing that stops you. As the **C.E.O. of your life**, this book is one of many tools you will have, along with the mindset, and the power to face fear and move past it. It's not about never feeling fear again, that's unrealistic. It's about recognizing fear for what it is: a temporary feeling, a distraction, and ultimately, something you can overcome.

Next time fear tries to tell you that you can't, remember this: **Fear is Fake Evidence Appearing Real.** It's not the truth. The truth is that you are capable, you are strong, and you have everything you need to succeed. And if not you are ready to go get the needed tools.

Embrace the discomfort of fear because it's a sign that you're growing. And growth is what we're here for. Growth doesn't happen when things are easy, it happens when you push past the fear and step into the unknown.

So go ahead. **Conquer fear.** Be bold. Be relentless. **Be the C.E.O. of your life**.

Figure 3.1 Your Turn: You're the C.E.O. Action Plan

Be Emboldened to Face Fear

Fear shows up in all of us, it's a natural response. But as the C.E.O. of your life, you are called to rise above it. Fear no longer controls you. Today, you take the lead. Let's remind ourselves that fear is just a trick our mind uses to protect us from the unknown, but growth doesn't happen in the known. It happens when you take that bold step into what's unfamiliar. As Lisa Nichols reminds us, *Fear is simply **"Fake Evidence Appearing Real."***

You've got the tools to move forward. **Clarity** in your actions, **Empowerment** through your choices, and **Ownership** of your direction. Embrace the fact that what might seem impossible today is really an opportunity to reprogram your mind and transform your future.

Here's your C.E.O. plan of action:

- **Identify the fear** that's holding you back, name it. What does it look like, sound like, and feel like?
- **Acknowledge it**, but don't let it dictate your next move. This fear isn't here to stay; it's here to be moved through.
- **Turn your past into power**. Every "no" you've ever heard, every setback, every obstacle, that's your foundation. Use it. You've overcome so much already, so what's one more fear to face?
- **Commit to brave action**. You don't need to be fearless to act; you just need to be brave enough to take one step forward. Every small step chips away at fear's power over you.

5-Minute Bravery Boost

Take five minutes, right now, to feel brave. Here's a quick activity to break through fear:

1. **Find a quiet space** and sit comfortably. Close your eyes and take three deep breaths. Inhale through your nose, exhale through your mouth. Let your body relax.
2. **Visualize a time** when you were scared but pushed through anyway. Maybe it was a job interview, a tough conversation, or stepping into a new role. Focus on that moment when you felt the fear but took action regardless. How did it feel to come out on the other side?
3. Now, **imagine the fear** you're facing today. What would it look like to move forward with bravery? Picture yourself taking that action, making the call, stepping into the room, launching that idea, and succeeding. Feel the pride and confidence in overcoming it.
4. **Write down one brave action** you can take today. Something small, but meaningful. A phone call, an email, setting a boundary, or saying "yes" to something you've been avoiding. Take that step within the next 24 hours. This action is your power move.

Fear may knock, but today you answer with courage. This is your moment to take control, to push forward, and to own the journey ahead. You are not here to shrink in the face of fear; you're here to rise above it.

Your Turn: CEO Affirmations

Affirmation 1:
"I embrace fear as a sign of growth. Every step I take is a step toward my greatness."

Affirmation 2:
"I am brave. I move with clarity and confidence, and nothing will stop me from achieving my goals."

Write them down, say them out loud, and let them fuel your next move. Fear can't stand a chance against the **C.E.O.** you're becoming!

Chapter 4: Creating an Action Plan

When I first laid out my plan, it wasn't perfect, but it was mine. And let me tell you something, it worked. I had my doubts, moments of confusion, and more than one late-night review of my notes, but when I hit my goal, the feeling was surreal. You know the type of victory that makes you stop, even for a second, in disbelief? That's where I was. I celebrated, yes, but part of me stood there stunned, asking myself, *Did I really do that?*

The success wasn't an accident. It came from those days, weeks, and months of refining my approach. From writing, rewriting, and checking my notes, to tweaking the plan and making adjustments on the fly. I didn't just want to win once, I wanted to replicate that success, time and time again.

As you grow, new challenges will emerge. And with each challenge, you'll have to stretch, move outside your comfort zone, and develop new strategies. You might feel like where you started was a lifetime ago, even though it's only been a few months. That's growth. And when you face new levels of growth, you need to be ready with a fresh action plan.

For me, that next-level action plan started with clarity. I began by putting my **"Y"** at the center of everything. If you don't know what's driving you, the plan won't hold up when things get tough. Everything I did, every task I undertook, had to align with my core reason for pursuing my goals. So I visualized it: my **"Y"** was in the center, and from it, each task branched out like spokes on a wheel. Everything led back to the reason I started.

Once I mapped it out, I created two columns for each task: **"What I Know"** and **"What I Need to Know."** This simple framework brought a level of clarity and focus I hadn't experienced before. It showed me where the gaps were, and from there, I could identify actionable steps to close them. And believe me when I tell you, there is always more you don't know until you dive in. Maybe that's why fear creeps in. It's the uncertainty that makes us hesitate. But let me tell you this: **don't let it stop you.** Once you get the right tools and information, you'll be a goal-achieving rockstar. In my *Nickelback* voice!

Building your plan is like constructing a house: you start with the foundation, the **Why** that keeps everything standing. Then, you design each room with a purpose, adding the details that turn it into something strong and sustainable. Here's how to build your blueprint:

- **Step One: Define Your Why**
  Everything starts here. If your goals don't align with your core reason for showing up, they'll fall apart. Your **Why** is what pushes you on the days you're tired, frustrated, or feeling like you're not making progress.
- **Step Two: Break Down the Goal**
  Once you have your Why, break your goal into actionable steps. Use a framework like S.M.A.R.T. (Specific, Measurable, Achievable, Relevant, Time-Based) to keep things clear and manageable.
- **Step Three: Identify What You Know vs. What You Need to Know**
  For each task, write down what you already know and what you still need to figure out. This brings clarity and allows you to prioritize learning or acquiring new skills to move forward.
- **Step Four: Celebrate the Small Wins**
  Don't wait for the big goal to give yourself credit. Celebrate each milestone along the way. It builds momentum and keeps you motivated.
- **Step Five: Adjust and Refine**
  The plan will need adjustments. Be ready to rework it as you

go. Growth requires flexibility, and sometimes the path changes along the way. That's okay, adapt and keep moving.

No plan can survive without the right tools and mindset to support it. Here's what you need in your toolbox to succeed:

- **A. The Most Essential Tool: An Open Mind**
  This journey will challenge you, and there will be times you don't know what to do. Keep your mind open to new ideas, perspectives, and possibilities. Growth doesn't happen with a closed mindset.
- **B. Ditch the Limiting Beliefs**
  The thought that you're not enough, not ready, or not worthy? Throw it out. You are enough today to start. Perfection is a myth, and waiting for everything to be just right will only hold you back.
- **C. Prepare for the Unexpected**
  Spoiler alert: things will not go as planned. Expect the unexpected, and when it shows up, roll with it. Challenges are part of the process, not an interruption of it.
- **D. Understand That Failure is Part of the Process**
  Fear of failure will try to stop you, but here's the truth: failure isn't the end. It's a tool for learning and refining your approach. Fail fast, learn fast, and keep pushing forward.
- **E. Perfection is a Myth**
  Stop striving for perfection. It doesn't exist. Progress is what matters. Move forward, even if it's imperfectly.

My Top 5 Books for Building Success

1. *The Seven Habits of Highly Effective People* by Stephen R. Covey
Covey's book taught me to think with the end in mind. Everything I do, from daily actions to long-term plans, starts with the vision of where I want to go.

2. *Rise and Grind* by Daymond John

This book taught me the value of dreaming big and working hard. You've got to be willing to put in the grind to make your dreams a reality.

3. *How to Own Your Own Mind* by Napoleon Hill

Hill's words hit home: if you don't own your emotions, you'll never own your thoughts. Master your emotions, and you'll master your mindset.

4. *Goals and Vision* by Les Brown

Les Brown taught me that anything I desire is possible. His book brought me the positivity I needed to keep moving forward, even when those around me weren't supportive.

5. *The Virgin Way* by Richard Branson

Branson showed me that life is about people and helping them reach their potential. Don't be afraid to be an outlier; that's where you'll find the most success.

Bonus Book: *Why Should White Guys Have All the Fun?* by Reginald F. Lewis

This book was a game-changer for me. Reginald F. Lewis, one of the first African American billionaires, taught me something profound: **it doesn't matter where you come from, who your parents are, or what society expects of you; you can create the life you want.**

Lewis' story of grit, intelligence, and unapologetic ambition showed me that the barriers we often face aren't as insurmountable as they seem. His tenacity in business, his ability to navigate a world that didn't always welcome him, and his boldness to ask, *Why should white guys have all the fun?* hit home for me.

What I learned from this book is that success isn't reserved for a select few, it's open to anyone with the drive and courage to take it. Your background, race, or circumstances don't define your ceiling. What defines you is how you take action, push through adversity, and own your journey.

Lewis' journey reminded me that we have the power to write our own narratives. If he could overcome the odds and create a legacy, so can we.

No one gets to the top alone. One of the most powerful tools in your arsenal is mentorship. Whether they are in your life physically or through books, mentors accelerate your growth, helping you avoid unnecessary mistakes and guiding you through challenges.

For me, as I wrote in **"Forged in Fire ~ From Ashes to Empowerment"** my early mentors came in the form of Sherlock Holmes and Bruce Wayne, fictional, yes, but they taught me that uniqueness is power. Holmes showed me the value of observation and deduction. Bruce Wayne, he taught me the importance of strategy and the courage to be different. These early lessons stayed with me. They shaped how I approach every obstacle and every goal.

As I progressed, I realized I needed more than just fictional mentors. I needed real-world guidance from those who had already walked the path. That's when I made a decision that changed everything. I took my last $300, swiped my credit card, and invested in a mentor. Was it scary? Absolutely. But that decision allowed me to learn from others' mistakes, accelerate my progress, and gain access to networks I wouldn't have had otherwise. I learned early on that **asking for help doesn't make you weak; it makes you strategic.**

Mentorship is about more than just advice. It's about having someone in your corner, someone who's already done what you're trying to do, and who can provide the roadmap and insight to get you there faster.

Figure 4.1 Your C.E.O. Action Plan: Defining Your "Why" and Building the Roadmap

It's time to put your C.E.O. cap on, Clarity in your actions, Empowered by your choices, and Owning your direction. Now, we're going to dive deeper into the core of what drives you: **your "Y"**. The reason behind your goals is what fuels your motivation and pushes you through the tough moments.

You've already identified your **"Y"** earlier in the book. But now, it's time to break it down even further. This is where we map out exactly **what you know** and **what you need to know** to move forward, because success isn't just about the passion, it's about the process. Let's clarify the path to make it actionable.

Breaking Down What You Know vs. What You Need to Know

Let's break it down side by side. On one side, list everything you already know related to your goal and journey. On the other side, list what you still need to learn or master. This helps us pinpoint exactly where you are and where you need to focus next.

What You Know   **What You Need to Know**

_____   _____

_____   _____

_____   _____

_____   _____

_____   _____

Now that you've laid it all out, look at your "What You Need to Know" column. That's your next target, these are the areas that need your attention, the gaps to fill to move closer to your "Y".

Taking Action: Your Top Priority

Pick the **top item** from your "What You Need to Know" column that's holding you back the most. This is the first step in closing the gap between where you are and where you want to be.

Write it down below as your top action item:

Top Item to Focus On:

_____

Breaking Down Your Action Steps

Now, we're going to break this top item into clear, actionable steps. Remember, no more overwhelm. As C.E.O., you create clarity from complexity by breaking things down piece by piece. Also you will not have all the steps in the beginning, move forward anyway!!

1. **First Step** – What's the first thing you can do to move closer to mastering this?

   _____

2. **Second Step** – What's next after that? Build on the first action.

   _____

3. **Third Step** – Continue the momentum. What comes after the second step?

   _____

4. **Fourth Step** – How will you know you've achieved this? What's your marker of success?

Time to Get In Action

You've created your steps, now it's time to execute. Remember, **progress over perfection.** Your only job now is to take the first step, then keep building on it.

When you've completed this task, take a moment to reflect on your progress. But don't stop there, **post your top goal in the CEO Habits Group** with the hashtag **#inaction** to let the community know you're moving forward.

Use this space to jot down your thoughts, steps, or any reflections as you go through the process:

_____
_____
_____
_____
_____

The power is in your hands. You're the C.E.O. of your life, and this is how we turn dreams into reality, by getting clear, building a plan, and **taking action**. Every time you step forward, you're redefining what's possible for yourself.

Remember, embracing the impossible isn't part of our vocabulary, the word itself says I'mPossible!

Chapter 5: The First Promotion - A Milestone Achieved

Promotion day arrived like a thunderclap, unexpected, exhilarating, and a bit terrifying. I had worked tirelessly, determined to stand out and make an impact. But this wasn't just a celebration of hard work paying off; it was a new chapter, full of responsibilities and challenges I hadn't fully anticipated. As the congratulations subsided, a deep realization set in: I was no longer just accountable for my own performance. Now, I was responsible for the team's morale, productivity, and their sense of purpose and growth. And, honestly, I was unprepared for what was ahead.

That initial promotion is a milestone we often set our sights on. It's the validation of our hard work and an affirmation that we're capable of more. For me, it was that and so much more. I had spent months pouring everything into my role, mastering every detail and going above and beyond to earn recognition. The hard work had its payoff, but little did I realize that stepping into this new role would be one of my hardest challenges yet. I had the skills to be a stellar worker, but a leader? That was different territory.

The first days on the job felt a bit surreal. My calendar suddenly filled with meetings, status updates, and strategy sessions. The weight of responsibility was immediate and heavy. I felt proud but deeply aware that my every action now had an impact on others. Not only was I responsible for ensuring productivity, but I was also tasked with creating a work environment that was supportive and motivating. Overnight, I'd become a mentor, a counselor, a coach, and, sometimes, even a parental figure. And, truthfully, I wasn't entirely sure I was ready for it.

There was a period where I found myself floundering. The demands were relentless, and I quickly learned that simply working harder wouldn't cut it. Leadership required more than just executing tasks; it demanded emotional intelligence, strategic thinking, and resilience in ways I hadn't anticipated. Yet, as disheartening as the first few weeks felt, I knew that this experience was just the beginning of my growth as a leader.

It wasn't long before reality hit me like a ton of bricks. My first few months in the role were riddled with complaints, misunderstandings, and fires to put out. The union was constantly on my back. The team wasn't connecting with my approach, and no amount of "do it this way" seemed to ease the situation. Every day was a juggling act where I barely managed to stay afloat, and I quickly found myself in reaction mode, trying to solve problems as they came instead of preventing them in the first place.

The burnout was fast and fierce, and by the end of that first two months, I knew something had to change. As the pressure mounted, I realized I couldn't keep going like this without seriously undermining my own potential and that of my team. In a humbling moment, I reached out to a senior manager who'd been through the trenches. I opened up about my struggles, admitting that I wasn't only overwhelmed by the workload but was struggling to help the team stop surviving and start thriving. He listened and then suggested that I attend a leadership training seminar.

The seminar itself was eye-opening, helping me understand more about what companies value in a leader, but it wasn't enough on its own. Real growth came when I returned to the office with a different mindset. I shifted my focus from problems to solutions. My ego had been trying to play the hero, saving the team from every challenge and jumping into action at every minor hiccup. But that wasn't what they needed. They needed clear communication, defined boundaries, and respect for their own strengths. They didn't need me to solve every problem; they needed me to guide them in finding solutions themselves.

One of the most transformative realizations was that leading wasn't about my own agenda, it was about theirs. I started meeting with department leads daily, listening deeply to understand their perspectives, needs, and the root of recurring issues. Gradually, we built a development plan together, one based on mutual respect and shared goals. The team was initially skeptical, but I encouraged them to try it and to provide feedback. After a few weeks, they not only adjusted to the new process but embraced it. We were finally moving forward as a unit, and for the first time, I felt like I was leading.

Through the struggle, I leaned on principles I would incorporate into the B.E.G.I.N. course. If I was going to be a successful leader, I had to embody certain principles fully.

The B.E.G.I.N. framework starts with building integrity, which for me meant a commitment to consistency. I needed to show up for my team every day, not just physically but with a focused mind and an open heart. And consistency wasn't just about being present but about following through on promises, setting a steady example, and demonstrating that success comes from doing the small things well day after day.

I focused on a concept I call the "7 Days of Integrity." I devoted seven days to tackling one issue at a time, slowly building my credibility with the team as they saw me work alongside them to address specific challenges. They began to realize that my intentions were genuine and that my commitment to their growth was unwavering. In return, they began to trust me, which was crucial for us to move forward together.

The introspection needed encouraged the techniques I placed into the B.E.G.I.N. framework also helped me see that I was part of the problem. My own habits and mental roadblocks were hindering me, and before I could effectively lead others, I had to confront my own shortcomings. The inner dive showed me that leading myself first would pave the way to becoming the leader my team needed.

I implemented the "Why and How" exercise I'd developed. I wrote my why at the center of a mind map and created branches for each task related to my goal. For each task, I made two columns: "What I Know" and "What I Need to Know." This approach helped me focus on actionable learning and development areas, allowing me to steadily accumulate the skills and insights I needed to grow.

Another critical principle that served me was that of empowerment. Empowerment isn't about giving people orders or instructions; it's about creating an environment where they feel capable of taking the initiative and solving problems on their own. I asked each team member to bring solutions, not just problems, to our discussions, emphasizing that they were integral to the success of our shared goals. Slowly, this mindset took root, and the team began to rise to challenges without waiting for direction.

Finally, I embraced the idea that growth is constant and that setbacks are part of the journey. We implemented regular check-ins to discuss progress, celebrate small wins, and re-evaluate strategies as necessary. This helped us keep momentum, even when things weren't perfect.

In hindsight, that first promotion was far more than just a step up the career ladder; it was the beginning of a deep, transformative journey. I learned that leadership is less about personal achievement and more about creating a path for others to succeed. The techniques were invaluable in guiding me through the rocky start, offering a roadmap for personal and professional growth. Leadership is about lifting others as you climb, and in that role, every small act, decision, and gesture becomes part of the legacy you leave behind.

If there's one lesson I could pass on from this experience, it's this: **Leadership isn't a title. It's a commitment to growth, resilience, and integrity.** It's an opportunity to shape your world and the lives of those around you. And with that commitment, every milestone becomes a stepping stone toward a future filled with greater impact and purpose.

Figure 5.1 It's Your Turn: "You're the C.E.O. Action Plan"

You're here because you know there's a leader within you, a voice, a vision, a presence that's ready to take charge and guide your life with purpose and clarity. But leading isn't just about setting goals or achieving milestones. It's about truly understanding what might be holding you back. So let's dive in and get introspective. This exercise is going to take you into a space where you'll explore what might be keeping you from fully stepping into the role of C.E.O. in your life.

Exercise: Identifying What Holds You Back from Leading

To get real about stepping into leadership, it starts with acknowledging where you're stuck. This process isn't about blame or shame, it's about awareness. Because once you're aware, you can take action. So, grab a pen, settle in, and let's dig in.

1. What's Keeping You From Leading?

First, take a deep breath. Clear your mind, and be honest with yourself as you answer these questions. Write down what comes to mind without filtering.

- What beliefs, fears, or habits are holding you back from leading confidently?

  Example answers: "I doubt my abilities," "I feel like I need more experience," or "I'm afraid of failing."

  _____

  _____

- What external factors, such as relationships, work environment, or obligations, do you feel are limiting your ability to lead in your life?
- *Example answers: "I'm surrounded by people who don't support my goals," or "I'm overcommitted and don't have time."*

_____

_____

2. What Would Leading Your Life Look Like?

Now that you've looked at what's holding you back, let's shift gears. Imagine if you had no obstacles in your way, what would your life look like if you were leading with intention, confidence, and vision? Write down your vision of leading your life.

- Describe what being the C.E.O. of your life looks like to you. How do you show up? What are your daily habits? How do you handle challenges?
  Example answers: "I make decisions based on my values," "I set clear goals for myself," or "I lead by example in everything I do."

_____

_____

3. Identify the First Action You'll Take

It's time to move from awareness to action. Look at what you've written down so far. Pick one thing you know you need to address, whether it's a limiting belief, a habit, or an external factor. This is your starting point.

- Write down the **one action** you're going to take this week to begin shifting that barrier. It doesn't have to be huge, it just has to be meaningful.

  Example answers: "I'll schedule 30 minutes every day to work on my personal goals," "I'll say no to one obligation that doesn't serve my purpose," or "I'll find one resource to help me strengthen my skills."

_____

_____

4. Reflection and Commitment

Let's lock it in. Write down your commitment to yourself. This is your promise to take action, no matter how small, every day as you step further into your role as C.E.O. of your life.

Example: "I commit to taking intentional action each day, breaking down barriers that hold me back, and embracing the leader I am meant to be."

_____

_____

Share with the Community:

Once you've completed your C.E.O. Action Plan, I encourage you to take it one step further. In the CEO Habits Group, share your top action for the week with the hashtag **#inaction**. Let's hold each other accountable, motivate each other, and celebrate the journey together.

You've got this, take the first step, and remember that every small action brings you closer to leading the life you deserve.

Chapter 6: Scaling New Heights Beyond the First Promotion

The first promotion was just the beginning. Once I broke through that initial barrier, something clicked. The upward momentum became a new normal, and over the next 14 months, I was promoted three more times. Each promotion represented more than just a new title, it was a testament to my growth and my ability to rise to new challenges, push beyond limitations, and continually expand what I thought was possible.

I found my niche, and that niche was leadership. It was a role that went beyond managing projects or people, it meant being the catalyst for growth, not just for myself but for everyone on the team. Leadership became the platform through which I could not only realize my own potential but also create opportunities for others to step into their greatness.

Every step was driven by my "Y", the reason I started this journey in the first place. It was simple yet powerful: to be a person my kids could be proud of. But as I grew, so did my "Y." It expanded beyond my family into my everyday interactions, into every room I walked into, and into the company I kept. I realized that to be the person my kids would look up to, I had to be someone who set an example of excellence, not just at home but in every aspect of life.

I needed to conduct myself differently, with intention and poise, adapting to each new role and responsibility. I became more intentional about the rooms I was in, the conversations I engaged in, and the way I responded to challenges. This growth became my mission, and it was the beginning of a new mindset, a blueprint for achieving success not just once, but continually, by setting new heights and scaling them.

The journey didn't end with that first promotion. In fact, it only got more intense. With every new role, the stakes were higher, the expectations greater, and the challenges tougher. But I had made a commitment to myself: I would continue to rise. Each promotion felt like a validation, yet it was also a reminder that I had a responsibility to keep growing, to keep setting higher goals, and to keep pushing the boundaries of what I could achieve.

So, I developed a resource, an e-book, **Dominating the Leg Up**, designed to help others replicate this process, to help them find their footing and thrive within their organizations. My readers have this book because they are ready to make that leap. For those who've purchased this book, email me at **Admin@jtdkbenterprises.com** with **Dominating the Leg Up** in the subject line, provide proof of purchase and I'll send you a free gift. It's my way of saying **Thank You** and helping others to start their journey toward their own "Y."

Each new promotion demanded that I hold myself to a higher standard, one that included continuous development and refinement. It wasn't just about achieving goals, it was about shaping myself into a leader who could handle any situation with poise and clarity. When challenging situations arose, I'd learned to respond with a solution-oriented mindset instead of reacting emotionally.

Reacting without control leads to problems; it can create an environment of fear, distrust, or even resentment. As a leader, I knew I had to remain composed, to be the steady hand in the storm, ready to provide answers and guide my team forward. Over time, this ability to respond rather than react became second nature, and it marked a turning point. It was the beginning of a new phase where I was truly in control, grounded in purpose, and ready to set and achieve higher goals continuously.

To truly succeed, I knew I needed to continually expand my skill set and grow my expertise. I dove back into my best teachers: books. But I didn't just read; I studied, I dissected, and I applied. I set a goal for myself: one book a week on leadership for an entire year. It wasn't just about soaking up information; it was about mastering a subject that I knew would be foundational to my growth and my ability to inspire others.

Each book offered new insights, new ways of thinking, and practical strategies that I could apply immediately. I took notes, applied the lessons, and refined my own approach. Leadership isn't something you learn once; it's something you practice, adapt, and evolve over time. The key is not just acquiring knowledge but applying it consistently. And as I did, I saw results, not just in my own performance but in the growth and confidence of the team around me.

The saying "knowledge is power" is only half-true. Real power comes from applied knowledge. It's what separates those who succeed from those who don't. I wasn't just learning leadership theories; I was putting them into practice, testing them in real situations, and seeing firsthand how they transformed both my work and the work of those around me. This application of knowledge was what fueled my growth and strengthened my resolve. I wasn't just accumulating facts, I was gaining real, actionable wisdom, and that made all the difference.

Each new achievement built my confidence. Confidence doesn't come from knowing all the answers; it comes from knowing that you can find the answers when you need them. It comes from experience, from testing yourself, and from proving to yourself that you're capable of handling whatever comes your way.

In the early days, I was afraid to fail. But I soon realized that failure is just a byproduct of taking chances, of being bold enough to step into the unknown. If you never fail, it's a sign you're not pushing hard enough, not taking risks. True leaders don't avoid failure, they embrace it as part of the journey, as proof that they're moving forward and growing.

Confidence isn't about never falling down; it's about knowing that you have the strength to get back up, to keep going no matter what. Every setback, every mistake, every obstacle became a stepping stone, an opportunity to learn, to grow, and to come back stronger. My motto became simple but powerful: potential is only realized when you're in action.

I also learned that leadership is not about being the smartest person in the room. Real leadership is about surrounding yourself with people who compliment your skills, who bring diverse perspectives and strengths to the table. I found confidence not in having all the answers but in knowing that I had a team around me that I could rely on, that I could learn from, and that I could trust.

The greatest lesson I've learned through this journey is that leadership is not about titles or positions. It's about influence, about making an impact, about helping others see their potential and inspiring them to pursue it. Each promotion was a step forward, yes, but it was also a responsibility, a call to grow not just myself but the people around me.

As I grew into leadership, I realized that the best way to lead is by example. I couldn't expect others to grow if I wasn't committed to my own growth. I couldn't ask others to strive for excellence if I wasn't willing to do the same. Leadership is about setting the standard, about being the model of what's possible. And as I did, as I lived out my values and my vision, I saw the team rise with me.

I developed a new mission for myself: to be a catalyst for growth, to help others see their own potential and to give them the tools to pursue it. This is the essence of leadership, the foundation upon which all my achievements have been built. And it's a journey I'm still on, a journey of continuous growth, of scaling new heights, and of helping others do the same.

For everyone reading this, I'm sharing these insights not just as my story but as a guide to help you on your own journey. Leadership isn't a destination, it's a path, a series of steps that you take each day. I believe in the power of mentorship, of sharing knowledge and experiences so that others can find their way forward with greater clarity and purpose.

If you're ready to take your own journey to the next level, to set new goals, to scale new heights, then let's do this together. Remember, the path to greatness isn't easy, but it's always worth it. And every step forward brings you closer to becoming the person you were meant to be, the leader you are capable of becoming.

As we wrap up this chapter, take a moment to reflect on your own journey. Where are you now? What are your goals? What are the steps you need to take to reach that next level? I invite you to set your sights higher, to challenge yourself, and to push beyond what you think is possible.

Leadership is not about arriving, it's about growing, about continually reaching for that next step, that next opportunity, that next milestone. You are capable of greatness. You are capable of being the leader not just in your career but in your life. Step into that role, embrace it, and own it. You're not just reading about scaling new heights, you're living it.

Figure 6.1 It's Your Turn: "You're the C.E.O. Action Plan"

Milestones are the markers of growth. They're the reminders that every step, no matter how big or small, is moving you closer to your goal. They're the points where you pause, reflect, and recognize what you've accomplished. And **yes**, each one deserves a celebration. This isn't just about pushing forward but also about creating a rhythm of progress and acknowledgment that fuels your journey.

In this action plan, you'll set clear milestone markers. These will be your personal checkpoints, places where you'll pause to take stock, recognize your efforts, and celebrate before moving to the next. Each milestone will come with a small yet meaningful activity to honor your progress.

This is your roadmap to becoming the C.E.O. of your life, **Creating Extraordinary Outcomes**. So let's begin. Set your sights on these milestones, track your progress, and celebrate each step forward. This is where your transformation begins.

Step 1: Define Your Milestones

1. **Set Three Milestones.**
   Think about the major stages in your journey. What are three key achievements that will mark real progress? These are the moments that will tell you you're moving in the right direction. They don't have to be the end goal, they can be smaller, manageable steps. The key is that they're meaningful to you. Take a moment to write down your three milestones.
   Milestone 1:

   _____
   Milestone 2:

   _____
   Milestone 3:

   _____

2. **Why These Milestones Matter.**
Reflect on why these milestones are important. What will achieving each one signify for you? Take time to connect with the purpose behind each milestone. When you know *why* it matters, staying motivated becomes much easier.

   ○ **Why Milestone 1 Matters:**
   _Write here:

   _____

   ○ **Why Milestone 2 Matters:**
   _Write here:

   _____

   ○ **Why Milestone 3 Matters:**
   _Write here:

   _____

Step 2: Create Your Celebration Activity

Each time you reach a milestone, plan an activity to celebrate your progress. Choose something that feels rewarding and rejuvenating. This isn't about extravagance, it's about acknowledgment. Every milestone celebration is a step in building confidence and resilience.

Celebration Ideas:

- Take yourself out for a coffee or a nice meal.
- Spend time doing something you love but don't often make time for.
- Write a letter to yourself celebrating the achievement.

For each milestone, decide on an activity that resonates with you and write it down here.

Celebration for Milestone 1:
_Activity: _____

Celebration for Milestone 2:
_Activity: _____

Celebration for Milestone 3:
_Activity: _____

Step 3: Reflect and Reinforce

When you reach each milestone, it's essential to reflect on the journey and reinforce the progress you've made. This is your time to be proud, to acknowledge how far you've come, and to use it as fuel for the next leg of the journey.

1. **What I Learned:**
   Take a moment to capture the most valuable lessons learned along the way. Each milestone reached comes with insights that will prepare you for the next challenge.
   Reflection for Milestone 1:
   _Write here:

   _____
   Reflection for Milestone 2:
   _Write here:

   _____
   Reflection for Milestone 3:
   _Write here:

   _____
2. **How I Grew:**
   Reflect on how achieving this milestone has helped you grow as a person, a leader, or a C.E.O. of your life. What new qualities or strengths have you developed?
   Growth for Milestone 1:
   _Write here:

   _____

Growth for Milestone 2:
_Write here:

Growth for Milestone 3:
_Write here:

---

3. **My Next Step:**
   Now that you've celebrated, it's time to set your sights on the next goal. Identify the immediate action you'll take next. It might be working on the next milestone or setting a new goal altogether.
   Next Step after Milestone 1:
   _Write here:

   Next Step after Milestone 2:
   _Write here:

   Next Step after Milestone 3:
   _Write here:

Final Words

Each milestone is a chapter in your journey, a step closer to realizing your full potential as the C.E.O. of your life. Remember, this isn't just a list, it's a reflection of your dedication, your resilience, and your commitment to **Creating Extraordinary Outcomes**. You're not just working toward a destination; you're building a legacy of growth, achievement, and purposeful action.

Now it's your turn. Go forward, reach each milestone, celebrate each win, and keep moving toward the life you've envisioned. This is your journey, and every step matters.

Chapter 7: Coming Full Circle to My "Y"

This all began on one cold January night, sitting on a front porch with the weight of the world on my shoulders. That night, I made a decision that changed everything,and realized my "Y." My purpose was clear: to be someone my kids could be proud of. It wasn't just a fleeting thought; it was the kind of realization that roots itself deep in your soul. From that moment on, my "Y" became the compass guiding every decision, every plan, and every sacrifice.

I spent countless hours reading, planning, re-evaluating, and working toward that goal. Every time doubt crept in, I went back to my "Y." It reminded me of what was at stake and kept me moving forward. Today, as I look at my now 26 and 27-year-old children, I know that I accomplished the main objective. They've grown into individuals with creativity, purpose, and integrity, and seeing them succeed brings me a sense of pride and fulfillment that words can't fully capture.

Let me be clear, it wasn't easy. Anything worth having isn't easy, but it is absolutely worth it. That cold night was the spark, but the fire required hard work, persistence, and resilience. There were moments of uncertainty and challenges that tested my resolve, but I refused to let them stop me.

The greatest moment of clarity came when my youngest wrote the introduction to my B.E.G.I.N. course. In that moment, I realized my "Y" had come full circle. My purpose wasn't just about making them proud, it was about showing them what was possible when you lead with purpose and determination. That realization wasn't just fulfilling; it was transformational. It became proof that living with a clear "Y" can inspire and uplift everyone around you.

Success isn't about titles, accolades, or bank accounts. True success is when your actions align with your core values.

Success without alignment is meaningless. It's fleeting, hollow, and unsustainable. I learned early on that for my success to be meaningful, it had to align with the values I held closest. Those values became my compass, guiding every decision and action. They were the foundation of my journey, the principles that kept me grounded when the road got rough.

Here are the core values I lived by:

1. **Integrity**
   Integrity was non-negotiable. For me, this meant doing what's right even when no one is watching. It meant keeping my word, treating others with respect, and staying true to my commitments. Every decision I made had to pass the integrity test: Does this align with who I say I am? Does it reflect the example I want to set for my kids?

2. **Resilience**
   Life will knock you down, that's a guarantee. But resilience is what allows you to get back up, dust yourself off, and keep moving forward. My resilience came from my "Y." No matter how hard things got, I reminded myself why I started. Resilience isn't about avoiding failure; it's about learning from it and using it as a stepping stone.

3. **Purpose**
   My purpose was clear: to inspire and uplift others, starting with my children. Purpose is what gave meaning to every late night, every tough decision, and every sacrifice. It's what kept me focused when distractions and doubts crept in. Purpose isn't just a feeling; it's a commitment to living intentionally.

4. **Excellence, Not Perfection**
   Excellence is about showing up every day and giving your best effort. It's about striving to be better than you were yesterday. I didn't aim for perfection because perfection is a myth. Instead, I aimed for progress, for steady improvement, for the kind of growth that comes from consistently doing the work.

5. **Service**

   True success isn't just about what you achieve, it's about how you help others along the way. I made it a point to lift as I climbed, to use my journey as a source of inspiration and empowerment for others. Service isn't just an act; it's a way of life.

It's about becoming the person you need to be to live a life that's meaningful and impactful. Core values are the foundation of everything, they guide your decisions, dictate your actions, and shape the legacy you leave behind.

I ask you to reflect on this: **Are you floating aimlessly through life, or are you taking charge?** I implore you to choose the latter. When you establish a core set of values to govern your life, every decision becomes clearer. You'll find yourself saying "no" to what doesn't align and "yes" to what pushes you toward your purpose. These values will become the compass that keeps you on course, even when the waters get rough.

For me, the shift came when I stopped drifting and started steering. My purpose became my anchor, and my core values became my guide. I made a commitment to live in my purpose daily. To be the change I wanted to see in the world. To lead with integrity, authenticity, and a relentless pursuit of excellence, not perfection, but excellence.

When I began holding myself and others to a higher standard, everything changed. I focused on being better than I was yesterday, on fostering growth and resilience within myself and those around me. It wasn't just about personal development,it was about creating ripples of change. I became the CEO of my life, taking ownership of my direction and influencing others to do the same.

Living this way has a transformative power. It starts with you, your mindset, your habits, your decisions, but it doesn't stop there. It spills over into your family, your community, and everyone you touch. That's the true impact of aligning success with your core values. It creates a chain reaction that inspires others to rise.

As I enter the next stage of my journey, I see the seeds of leadership being planted in others. I see individuals stepping into their own power, unapologetic and unwavering in their determination to make an impact. Watching new leaders find their voice and pave their own paths is one of the most rewarding parts of this journey. It's a reminder that the work I've done is about more than personal success, it's about creating a legacy of empowerment and growth.

For my children, their journey looks different than mine, and that's exactly how it should be. The world they're building for themselves is unique, shaped by their own passions, goals, and experiences. Different doesn't mean wrong; it simply means it's theirs. My hope for them is that they, too, have a "Y" big enough to guide them through life's inevitable challenges. They will stumble and fall, as we all do, but I know they'll rise because they've seen firsthand the value of resilience and purpose.

Failure isn't something to be avoided, it's a stepping stone to success. My "Y" has taught me that stumbling blocks are simply part of the journey, and the only way to fail is to stop moving. I've designed the B.E.G.I.N. course to provide mentorship and guidance for those navigating their own paths. It's a tool to help others find their footing, build their confidence, and take charge of their lives.

As I continue to grow and evolve, my focus shifts to sustaining and expanding my impact. I'm committed to leaving a legacy that goes beyond financial success, a legacy rooted in empowerment, leadership, and transformation. This means staying active in my community, mentoring the next generation of leaders, and continuing to develop tools and resources that make personal and financial growth accessible to everyone.

Sustaining success requires intentionality. It's not enough to achieve your goals; you have to nurture and build upon them. For me, this involves a mix of financial strategies, personal development initiatives, and exploring new ventures. I continue to invest in real estate, leveraging my portfolio to create both financial security and opportunities for others. But financial growth is only one piece of the puzzle.

Personal development remains a cornerstone of my journey. I prioritize lifelong learning, attending seminars, networking with other leaders, and investing in my own growth. Staying curious and open to new ideas allows me to adapt and innovate as I scale my impact.

New ventures also play a critical role. Whether it's launching a new course, writing a book, or collaborating with other leaders, I'm always looking for ways to expand my reach and make a difference. Every new project is an opportunity to create value, inspire others, and reinforce the principles that have guided me from the beginning.

Coming full circle to my "Y" has been a journey of clarity, fulfillment, and continuous growth. What began as a simple desire to make my kids proud has evolved into a mission to inspire and empower others. My "Y" has transformed not only my life but the lives of those around me. It has become a guiding light, a beacon of hope, and a source of strength.

This purpose isn't just something I hold, it's something I share. It's the foundation of my work, my relationships, and my legacy. And as I move forward, I'm more committed than ever to living in alignment with my "Y," to leading with integrity, and to helping others discover the power of their own purpose.

Figure 7.1 It's Your Turn: "You're the C.E.O. Action Plan"

Understanding and Creating Your Core Values

As the C.E.O. of your life, your **core values** are your compass. They guide your decisions, govern your actions, and ensure you're always aligned with the person you aspire to be. Without clear values, you risk drifting, making choices that don't serve your purpose, or settling for less than you deserve. But when your values are clear, every action you take is intentional, purposeful, and aligned with your "Y."

Today, it's your turn to define the core values that will shape your journey. These are the principles that will anchor you during challenges, inspire you during uncertainty, and remind you who you are when the road gets tough. Let's create the foundation that will govern your actions and keep you moving toward the life you're building.

Step 1: Reflect on What Matters Most

Take a moment to think about what truly matters to you. Your core values should reflect the qualities, beliefs, and priorities that define who you are and who you want to become. Answer these questions to start uncovering your values:

- What qualities do I admire most in others?
  (Example: integrity, resilience, empathy, courage)

  _____

  _____

- When I think about my best moments, what values were present?
  (Example: hard work, honesty, determination)

  _____

  _____

- What do I want to be known for?
  (Example: uplifting others, living with purpose, being dependable)

  _____

  _____

Step 2: Define Your Core Values

Now that you've reflected, it's time to name your values. Write down 3–5 core values that will serve as the foundation for your actions. These are the principles you'll live by and use to guide every decision you make.

1. _____
2. _____
3. _____
4. _____
5. _____

Step 3: Align Your Actions with Your Values

A value is just a word until you bring it to life through action. Take each value you've written and think about how you'll honor it in your daily life. Answer the following for each core value:

- **How will I embody this value every day?**
  (Example: For integrity, you might commit to being honest in every interaction, even when it's uncomfortable.)

1. _____
2. _____
3. _____

- **What actions align with this value?**
  (Example: For service, you might look for ways to uplift others in your community or workplace.)

1. _____
2. _____

3. _____

_____

Step 4: Commit to Living Your Values

Write a personal commitment to yourself. This is your promise to live in alignment with your values, to let them govern your actions, and to use them as a guide for every step of your journey.

My Commitment:
"I commit to living in alignment with my core values. I will let them guide my decisions, govern my actions, and inspire me to be the best version of myself. I understand that my values are my foundation, and I will honor them daily as I build the life I deserve."

_____

_____

_____

Final Step: Share Your Core Values

Accountability and community can strengthen your commitment. Share your top core value in the CEO Habits Group with the hashtag **#MyCoreValues** and inspire others to reflect on their own.

Remember, as the C.E.O. of your life, your values are your compass. Keep them at the forefront of your journey, and they'll lead you to a life of purpose, alignment, and fulfillment. **This is your foundation. Own it.**

Chapter 8: Break the Chains to Gain

Breaking the chains isn't just about overcoming your past; it's about using every opportunity in your present to build the life you envision. In this chapter, we're diving into how you leverage your job as an investor in your future, develop strategies for real estate, build multiple streams of income, and sustain your success for the long haul. This isn't just about reaching six figures, it's about breaking the ceiling, creating generational wealth, and gaining financial freedom.

When we talk about your job being your best investor, we're not just talking about 401(k)s, IRAs, or other structured benefits, though those are valuable tools for your future. We're talking about shifting your perspective. Instead of seeing your employer as someone you work for, see them as an investor funding your next level.

Up and to this point you've developed the CEO tools, techniques, and skillset to thrive in your role and beyond. Now, it's time to use your position to fuel your bigger dreams, whether it's investing in real estate, starting a business, or building wealth through stocks or crypto. Your job is your training ground, your incubator, and your financial foundation.

You are not just an employee, you are an investment. When I say you are an investment, I mean that **you are valuable to your employer**. Your skills, dedication, and contributions are assets that drive the success of the organization. Companies invest time, resources, and training into you because they see your potential and believe in your ability to deliver results.

This isn't about feeling used, it's about recognizing the value you bring to the table and leveraging that value to grow both professionally and personally. You're not just an employee; you're a key player in achieving the company's mission. And as you add value to the organization, you're also building a foundation for your future.

By seeing yourself as an investment, you step into a position of empowerment, understanding that your growth within the company aligns with the growth of your own skills, knowledge, and opportunities. This is your chance to maximize every resource available to you, strengthening your journey toward achieving your goals. **You are essential, capable, and worthy of investing in, not just by others, but by yourself.**

Take my journey as an example. For over 25 years, I leveraged every opportunity at my job to grow my expertise in leadership, process management, and strategic planning. Everything I learned became the foundation for starting my coaching and leadership academy, *Say I'mPossible Academy*. The processes, SOPs, and hiring practices I implemented for my employer became the tools I used to scale my own business.

As you grow within your career, remember: the endgame isn't just survival until retirement. It's about asking yourself, What's my plan when I call it quits? Many dive straight into entrepreneurship without a clear roadmap, going from working for a check to working to build a check. Use your job to absorb the knowledge you'll need to succeed as a business owner, investor, or leader in any field. That way, you start with a head start instead of stumbling into unnecessary failures.

As I advanced in my career, I began stepping into new circles, rooms where the conversations were no longer about surviving but thriving. In these spaces, one topic consistently came up: real estate.

At the time, I had a couple of properties, but these individuals were talking about owning hundreds of "doors." In real estate, every door represents cash flow, and these investors had elevated the Monopoly game of childhood to real life. I understood that just like in the game, success comes from buying the right properties, the ones people will always stop at, the ones that generate profit.

Rule #1 in Real Estate: Buy right to make a profit.

That lesson sparked my deeper dive into real estate. I reached out to an investor I'd worked with years earlier when I ran a cleaning service specializing in pre-renovation properties. My first question to them was simple: How can I be of service? My second: Can I ask questions along the way?

This approach allowed me to gain firsthand knowledge while providing value. I started wholesaling properties, a strategy that involves working with property owners to secure a deal and then selling the contract to an investor for a profit. Wholesaling gave me insight into the market, investor needs, and the critical factors that make a property valuable.

But here's the most important part: I operated with integrity. I wasn't just looking for deals, I was providing solutions. I helped property owners navigate challenging situations, offering resources even when it meant they kept their properties. Integrity is the foundation of every successful investment, and it became my guiding principle.

Wealth isn't just about making more money. It's about understanding currency, how money flows, grows, and works as a tool for freedom. For me, building wealth started with education. Books like Rich and Righteous by Jullien Gordon and The One Week Budget by Tiffany Aliche reshaped how I thought about finances. They taught me that money isn't just a resource; it's a reflection of how we value ourselves and our time.

The key to wealth-building is diversification. I knew I needed multiple income streams, but that wasn't just about throwing money into random ventures. It required introspection. I asked myself:

- What are my strengths?
- How can I use them to serve others?
- What aligns with my values and goals?

From there, I identified three key areas where I excelled and began turning those into income streams. Here's the process I followed:

- Write What You Know: List everything you already understand deeply.
- Write What You Need to Learn: Identify gaps in your knowledge and skills.
- Start with What You Know Best: Begin with the area you're most comfortable in to build momentum and confidence.

Your talents are your greatest form of currency. When you turn your knowledge into marketable products or services, you create opportunities not just for income but for impact.

I also ensured my 4-S framework—Self-Esteem, Self-Discipline, Self-Care, and Self-Awareness—remained aligned. These pillars helped me stay balanced, avoiding burnout while expanding my income streams. Wealth isn't just about accumulation; it's about using your resources wisely and maintaining harmony in your life.

Building wealth is only half the equation. Sustaining it requires strategy, discipline, and a long-term mindset. This isn't a sprint; it's a marathon, and marathons require preparation, endurance, and adaptability.

I approached this chapter of my life by immersing myself in seminars, networking events, and courses. Success is dynamic, it evolves as you grow. To sustain it, you need to keep leveling up your knowledge and adapting to the changing landscape.

Here are my long-term strategies for sustaining success:

- Build a Team of Experts: Surround yourself with financial advisors, lawyers, and professionals who can guide you. No one succeeds alone.
- Continue Learning: I passed real estate and insurance exams to deepen my understanding of these industries. Knowledge is an ongoing investment.
- Strategic Growth: Focus not just on acquiring assets but on optimizing and growing them. Whether it's real estate, businesses, or stocks, every decision should align with your long-term vision.
- Protect Your Wealth: Invest in insurance, estate planning, and risk management to safeguard your assets for the future.

Success is not just about achieving a certain income or status, it's about building a legacy. It's about creating something that lasts, something that continues to grow and provide value long after you've reached your initial goals.

Breaking the chains to gain is about more than just reaching six figures. It's about using every resource, your job, your skills, your investments, to create a life of freedom and purpose. It's about understanding that you are not just an employee, investor, or leader, you are the architect of your future.

As you move forward, remember that this is your journey. Whether it's leveraging your job as an investor, diving into real estate, creating multiple income streams, or sustaining your success, every step you take brings you closer to your goals. The key is action. Potential is realized in motion, and your next level is waiting for you to step into it.

You have the tools. You have the vision. Now, it's time to break the chains and gain.

Figure 8.1 It's Your Turn: "You're the C.E.O. Action

Determining What Your Next Level Looks Like

As the C.E.O. of your life, it's time to think beyond where you are now. Success isn't just about climbing the career ladder or hitting financial milestones, it's about creating freedom. Freedom to live the life you envision, retire with confidence, and leave a legacy that matters. But freedom doesn't just happen, it's built intentionally, one stream of income at a time.

In this action plan, you'll define what your next level looks like and explore the income streams that will sustain your future. This isn't about wishful thinking, it's about actionable clarity. Let's dive in and map out the path to your financial freedom.

Step 1: Visualize Your Next Level

Take a moment to visualize what freedom looks like for you. What does retirement mean in your life? Is it traveling the world, spending more time with family, or running a business you're passionate about? The clearer your vision, the more focused your plan will be.

Answer these questions to get started:

What does financial freedom mean to me?

_Write here:

_____

What does my ideal life in retirement look like?

_Write here:

_____

What legacy do I want to leave behind?

_Write here:

_____

Step 2: Identify Your Strengths and Opportunities

Freedom comes from diversification—multiple streams of income that sustain and grow over time. But these income streams should align with your strengths, passions, and opportunities.

List Your Strengths:

What skills, knowledge, or talents do you have that could generate income?

_Write here:

_____

Explore Opportunities:

What industries, markets, or ventures interest you?

_Write here:

_____

Match Your Strengths to Opportunities:

Circle the ones that align with what you're good at and passionate about.

Step 3: Map Out Your Income Streams

Now that you've identified your strengths and opportunities, it's time to brainstorm potential income streams. These could include real estate investments, stocks, businesses, side hustles, or even passive income from intellectual property like books or courses.

Use this space to outline the possibilities:

Stream 1: _____

Why this stream? _____

First steps to start: _____

Stream 2: _____

Why this stream? _____

First steps to start: _____

Stream 3: _____

Why this stream? _____

First steps to start: _____

Stream 4: _____

Why this stream? _____

First steps to start: _____

Step 4: Create a Freedom Timeline

Now that you have your income streams mapped out, it's time to set some milestones. Think about when you want each stream to start generating income and how much you want each to contribute.

Stream 1 Goal Date: _____

Income Goal: _____

Stream 2 Goal Date: _____

Income Goal: _____

Stream 3 Goal Date: _____

Income Goal: _____

Stream 4 Goal Date: _____

Income Goal: _____

Step 5: Plan to Celebrate and Share

Every step toward financial freedom is worth celebrating. Write down how you'll reward yourself when you hit your first income stream goal.

My Celebration Plan:

_Write here:

_____

_____

When you hit a milestone, share your success in the CEO Habits Group with the hashtag **#FreedomInAction** to inspire others to take charge of their journey.

You are in control of your future, and your next level is within reach. This plan isn't just a list, it's the foundation of your freedom. By diversifying your income, leveraging your strengths, and taking intentional action, you're creating a life that's not just about surviving but thriving.

Let's get to work, your future self is waiting for you to step up. You've got this!

Chapter 9: Mentorship and Community

Mentorship and community are two of the most powerful tools for growth. No matter how much we achieve on our own, there's a limit to what one person can do in isolation. When we give back, create support networks, and inspire others, we don't just elevate those around us, we elevate ourselves.

The most important part of growing, learning, and developing is helping others do the same. It's not just about what we achieve, it's about what we pour into others so they, too, can grow and thrive. I realized early in my career that I couldn't give from an empty cup. Not successfully anyway. Trying to help others while constantly worrying about making ends meet was draining, and I knew I needed to change that.

When I started to build stability in my own life, I understood that the assignment wasn't just to grow for myself. It was to become an example, to show others what's possible, and to lift them as I climbed. Giving back wasn't optional, it was essential. As I learned more, I taught more. As I overcame obstacles, I reached back to help others navigate theirs. Mentorship became not just something I did, but a core part of who I am.

Coming from the cold streets, as I wrote about in **Forged In Fire: From Ashes to Empowerment**, I know how difficult it is to escape the grip of struggle. Those experiences shaped me. They left scars, but they also taught me lessons, harsh, valuable lessons that built my resilience and shaped my perspective. I don't mentor people by saying, "Look at what I've achieved." I mentor them by saying, "Look at what I've survived." That's what resonates. Not the polished image of success, but the gritty truth of the journey it took to get there.

When I speak at events, I share those truths. I talk about what it felt like to wonder if I could ever break free. I talk about the action plans I created, the goals I set, and the relentless work I put in to turn those plans into reality. Most importantly, I remind people that success isn't reserved for the lucky or the chosen few. It's for anyone willing to put in the work.

My favorite moments as a mentor are the ones where I see the light of hope cross someone's face. That spark, when someone begins to believe that their dreams are possible, that's why I mentor. It's not just about teaching skills or sharing knowledge. It's about helping people see the potential within themselves, the power they've always had but didn't recognize. That's the magic of mentorship.

I mentor for the little boy or girl at home, dreaming in silence because no one is listening. I mentor for the warehouse worker, the cashier, the clerk, the entry level team member who feels stuck but has a fire burning deep inside. To them, I say this: Start today. Write your action plan. Shift your mindset toward success. You have the power to change your circumstances, and when you do, you'll inspire others to do the same.

Success doesn't happen in isolation. Surrounding yourself with the right people is just as important as having the right plan. You've probably heard the saying: *You are the average of the five people you spend the most time with.* I believe this wholeheartedly, and it's why I've always been intentional about building a network of like-minded individuals who inspire, uplift, and challenge me to be my best.

When I started creating the B.E.G.I.N. program, I didn't just want to build a coaching framework, I wanted to create a community. A space where people could mastermind, share ideas, and support one another. Why? Because our thoughts don't exist in isolation. They permeate our minds and shape our surroundings. If you're surrounded by negativity, doubt, and fear, those things will seep into your actions. But when you're surrounded by positivity, encouragement, and growth-minded individuals, you're empowered to reach new heights.

Creating a support network isn't just about finding people who agree with you, it's about finding people who challenge you, who push you to grow, and who hold you accountable to your goals. It's about building relationships based on mutual respect, shared values, and a commitment to helping each other succeed.

In my mentorship journey, I've worked hard to foster this kind of environment. I bring together leaders who not only appreciate your thoughts but amplify them. Leaders who see the best in you and encourage you to strive for it. This kind of inclusion is empowering. It gives you the confidence to take bold steps because you know you're supported by people who believe in you.

Building this kind of network requires intentionality. Here's what I've learned:

- **Be Selective About Who You Let In**: Your circle should reflect your values and your goals. Surround yourself with people who inspire you, challenge you, and support your growth.
- **Give as Much as You Take**: A strong network is built on reciprocity. Be willing to support others in their journeys, just as they support you in yours.
- **Stay Engaged**: Relationships require effort. Stay connected, offer encouragement, and celebrate each other's wins.

When you build and nurture a strong network, you create a safety net of inspiration and accountability. You're never alone on the journey, and that support can make all the difference.

There's power in sharing your story. Not the polished, picture-perfect version of success, but the real, raw journey that got you there. When we share our challenges, our failures, and our victories, we remind others that they're not alone. We show them that success isn't about perfection, it's about persistence.

In my speeches, my books, and my mentorship, I make it a point to be transparent about my journey. I talk about the times I doubted myself, the nights I stayed up worrying, and the moments I thought about giving up. Why? Because those moments are where growth happens. Those moments are where resilience is built.

When people see someone who's been where they are, who's faced the same struggles and come out stronger, it gives them hope. It reminds them that they, too, can overcome whatever they're facing. That's the gift of sharing your story, it turns your scars into a roadmap for someone else.

But inspiring others isn't just about telling your story, it's about showing them what's possible. It's about being an example of what happens when you refuse to settle, when you take control of your life, and when you commit to living in alignment with your purpose.

One of the most rewarding parts of my journey has been hearing from people who've been inspired by my work. They tell me that my story gave them the courage to take the first step toward their own dreams. That's what it's all about, using your journey to light the way for others.

Mentorship and community are the lifeblood of growth. They remind us that we're not alone, that we're stronger together, and that we all have the power to inspire and uplift one another. Giving back, creating support networks, and sharing our stories aren't just acts of generosity, they're acts of empowerment.

As you reflect on your journey, I encourage you to think about how you can give back, build your network, and share your story. Who can you mentor? Who can you connect with to create a supportive environment for growth? What parts of your journey can you share to inspire someone else?

The power is within you to make these choices. You have the ability to realign your path and help others do the same. Remember: mentorship isn't just about guiding others, it's about growing together. And when you create a community built on trust, respect, and shared purpose, there's no limit to what you can achieve.

Let's keep building, growing, and lifting each other up. Together, we're unstoppable.

Figure 9.1 It's Your Turn: "You're the C.E.O. Action Plan"

Why Your Story Matters: Learning from the Moment and Letting Go

Every story matters, especially yours. Your story is more than a series of events; it's a blueprint of your growth, resilience, and power. But too often, we hold on to the wrong parts of our story. We relive mistakes, carry guilt, or let the weight of past moments define our future. Let me remind you: **your story doesn't hold you back, it fuels your growth, but only if you learn from it and let it guide you forward.**

This is where the **4 Pillars of Self**: Self-Awareness, Self-Esteem, Self-Care, and Self-Discipline, come into play. Today, we're focusing on **Self-Awareness**: the ability to reflect on your story, extract its lessons, and release what no longer serves you. Your story isn't a prison, it's your power. Let's uncover why it matters and how you can learn from the moment without holding on to the weight of it.

Step 1: Why Your Story Is Important

Your story has shaped you. It's the foundation of who you are today, but it's not the whole picture. Reflect on why your story matters. What has it taught you about resilience, strength, and growth? How has it prepared you for where you're headed?

Write down why your story is important and how it has shaped your journey so far.

Why My Story Matters:

1. _____
2. _____
3. _____

Step 2: 3 Lessons to Learn from Your Story

Let's focus on the lessons your story has to offer. Every experience, good or bad, has something to teach you. Use these three questions to uncover the lessons hidden within your story.

1. **What Strength Did I Discover?**
   Even in the hardest moments, you've shown resilience. What strengths have emerged because of what you've been through?
   My Strength:

   _____

2. **What Pattern Do I Need to Break?**
   Sometimes, our story reveals habits or cycles that no longer serve us. What patterns do you need to let go of to move forward?
   Pattern to Break:

   _____

3. **What Lesson Can I Use to Empower Others?**
   Your story isn't just for you, it can inspire and uplift others. What lesson from your journey can you share to make a difference?
   Lesson to Share:

   _____

Step 3: Letting Go Without Losing the Lesson

Learning from your story doesn't mean holding on to it forever. It means taking the lessons and releasing the pain, guilt, or fear that no longer serve you. Here's a tool to help you let go:

The Release and Empowerment Exercise

- Write down one thing from your story that you're ready to release.
- Then, write one way you'll use the lesson from that experience to move forward.

What I'm Releasing:

_____

How I'll Use the Lesson:

_____

_____

Step 4: Your C.E.O. Commitment

Self-awareness is the foundation of growth, but it only works if you're willing to take action. Write a commitment to yourself. This is your promise to learn from your story, let go of what no longer serves you, and use your journey as fuel for your future.

My Commitment:
"I commit to honoring my story by learning from it and letting it guide me forward. I will release what holds me back and use my journey to inspire myself and others. My story is my power, and I choose to own it."

_____

_____

Final Step: Share Your Strength

Your story is a gift. It's proof that growth is possible and that setbacks are just setups for something greater. Share one strength or lesson you've learned from your story in the **CEO Habits Group** with the hashtag **#MyStoryIsPower** to inspire others on their journey.

Remember, as the C.E.O. of your life, your story is your power. Learn from it, grow through it, and let it propel you into your next chapter. **You're in charge, now own it.**

Chapter 10: The Journey Continues

As I sit here, reflecting on my journey from a poverty mindset to financial success, I'm overwhelmed by a mix of emotions, gratitude, pride, and a deep sense of purpose. This isn't just my story; it's a testament to what's possible when you refuse to let your circumstances define you. Looking back, I can see how every setback, every challenge, and every triumph shaped the person I am today.

I didn't grow up with a silver spoon or a roadmap to success. My story began on the cold streets, in the uncertainty of wondering how I'd make it through another day. But even in those moments, there was a fire inside me, a belief, however faint, that life could be different. That belief became my fuel.

The journey wasn't linear. There were moments of doubt, days when I felt like giving up, and times when the weight of responsibility felt too heavy to carry. But each of those moments taught me something. They taught me resilience, patience, and the importance of persistence. They taught me that success isn't about having it all figured out, it's about taking one step forward, even when the path ahead isn't clear.

One of the most pivotal shifts for me was understanding the power of mindset. Poverty isn't just a lack of money; it's a mindset that convinces you that what you have is all you'll ever get. Breaking free from that mindset was one of the hardest, yet most transformative, parts of my journey. I had to reprogram my thoughts, replace doubt with belief, and focus on what I could achieve instead of what I lacked.

From that shift came action. I set goals, created plans, and executed them relentlessly. I educated myself, surrounded myself with people who inspired and challenged me, and built habits that aligned with my aspirations. I learned to see failure not as an endpoint but as a lesson, a stepping stone to something greater.

Now, as I reflect on the milestones, the promotions, the financial growth, the investments, and the opportunities to mentor and inspire others, I realize that the greatest success isn't what I've achieved but who I've become. And the best part? This journey isn't over. In many ways, it's just beginning.

The journey to financial success and personal growth is ongoing. It doesn't stop when you hit six figures, buy your first property, or achieve a major milestone. In fact, those achievements are just the foundation for what comes next. As I look to the future, my goals are bigger than ever, not just for myself, but for the people I serve.

1. Expanding My Impact
One of my primary goals is to continue empowering others to break free from limiting beliefs and achieve their own success. Through mentorship, the B.E.G.I.N. program, and the communities I've built, I want to reach more people, helping them see that their dreams are within reach. Whether it's the young woman feeling stuck in a dead-end job or the single parent wondering how to make ends meet, my mission is to show them that transformation is possible.

2. Growing My Financial Portfolio
On a personal level, I'm focused on growing my real estate portfolio and exploring new investment opportunities. But it's not just about wealth accumulation, it's about creating generational wealth. I want to leave a legacy that provides not just for my children but for their children, too. This means continuing to educate myself, staying adaptable to changes in the market, and making strategic decisions that align with my long-term vision.

3. Developing New Tools and Resources
I'm passionate about creating practical tools and resources that help

others on their journey. Whether it's writing more books, developing online courses, or hosting live workshops, my goal is to provide actionable guidance that people can use to change their lives. I want to take what I've learned and make it accessible to as many people as possible.

4. Prioritizing Personal Growth

Success isn't just about external achievements; it's also about internal growth. As I continue this journey, I'm committed to deepening my self-awareness, strengthening my relationships, and cultivating a life that feels fulfilling on every level. That means setting boundaries, practicing self-care, and continuing to challenge myself to evolve as a leader, mentor, and individual.

Final Thoughts: Your Journey Begins Here

If there's one thing I want you to take away from this book, it's this: **You have the power to change your life.** No matter where you're starting from, no matter how many obstacles are in your way, you are capable of achieving more than you can imagine. The tools, strategies, and stories I've shared throughout this book are proof that transformation is possible.

But here's the thing: reading about it isn't enough. You have to act. You have to take the knowledge you've gained and put it into practice. You have to make the decision, right now, that you're going to show up for yourself every single day. Because success doesn't happen by accident, it happens by design.

Your journey won't look exactly like mine, and it shouldn't. Your path is unique to you, shaped by your dreams, your challenges, and your "Y." But what's universal is the process: setting goals, creating a plan, and committing to consistent action. It's about embracing the lessons in every setback, celebrating every small win, and staying focused on the bigger picture.

As you embark on this journey, remember that you're not alone. There's a community of people, myself included, who are cheering for you, supporting you, and ready to walk alongside you. Lean into that support. Surround yourself with people who inspire you, challenge you, and hold you accountable to your potential.

And when the road gets tough, and it will, come back to your "Y." Let it remind you why you started. Let it reignite the fire inside you and give you the strength to keep going. Because the truth is, the only thing standing between you and the life you want is your willingness to take the first step.

This isn't just about achieving success for yourself, it's about creating a legacy. It's about showing the people around you, your family, your friends, your community, that it's possible to rise above your circumstances. It's about inspiring the next generation to dream bigger, work harder, and believe in their own potential.

As I continue my journey, I'm committed to doing just that. I'm committed to giving back, sharing what I've learned, and using my story to empower others to write their own. But now it's your turn. It's your turn to take the tools, strategies, and lessons from this book and apply them to your life. It's your turn to take control, set your goals, and start building the life you deserve.

The journey from poverty to financial success isn't easy, but it's worth it. It's worth every sacrifice, every late night, and every moment of doubt. Because on the other side of those challenges is a life that's bigger, bolder, and more fulfilling than you ever imagined.

You have everything you need within you. You have the strength, the resilience, and the determination to succeed. Now it's time to take action. The journey continues, and I can't wait to see where it takes you. Let's build something extraordinary together.

Remember: You are the C.E.O. of your life. Own it. Lead it. Live it.

Tools From the Author:

"The Say I'mPossible Academy".

My offerings aren't just products, they are blueprints for building the life you deserve, crafted with care and designed to empower you step by step.

The B.E.G.I.N. Course
This is where transformation begins. If you're ready to step into your power and become the CEO of your life, the B.E.G.I.N. course is your launchpad. We'll cover everything from building rock-solid habits to defining the mindset you need to crush your goals. It's more than just lessons, it's a system designed to get you results. Whether you're looking to level up in your career or your personal life, this course lays the foundation to get you there, one intentional step at a time.

E-Book: Dominating the Leg-up
For those navigating their way into leadership, *Dominating the Leg-up* gives you the playbook to thrive in any competitive environment. This e-book breaks down practical strategies to take your career to the next level by owning your strengths, leveraging your network, and mastering the habits that separate good from great. It's a fast-paced guide packed with actionable insights.

E-Book: Living There, Be Aware
In the world of real estate, being a successful investor requires more than just finding a property, it's about being the CEO of your decisions. *Living There, Be Aware* is designed to guide you through the process of buying an investment property with clarity, empowerment, and ownership of your future. Before you even step into the market, you'll learn how to identify your specific needs, wants, and desires for your next property, ensuring that every move you make aligns with your long-term goals.

This e-book is packed with practical checklists and advice on how to pick the right key players in your investment journey. From selecting the best realtors, loan officers, and general contractors, to finding consultants who truly understand your vision, it helps you build the ultimate team to guarantee success. By the time you finish, you won't just be buying a property, you'll be making a strategic investment that supports the life and future you're creating.

The E.P.I.C.(Elevate Potential to Ignite Change) Collection

Part I: Forged In Fire ~ From Ashes to Empowerment

This is a transformative guide that turns life's toughest challenges into stepping stones for success. Through real-life stories and actionable strategies, this book empowers you to reclaim your power, break free from limitations, and rise stronger than ever. It's time to embrace your resilience and ignite the fire within!

Part II: #Poverty_to_6_figures ~ Break the Chains to Gain

This isn't just a story of making it out of poverty, it's a blueprint for how you can, too. *#Poverty_to_6_Figures* is my journey from $7-an-hour jobs to multiple six-figure successes in real estate and entrepreneurship. I break down every key lesson learned along the way so you don't just see the end result, you get the strategies to make it happen for yourself. It's raw, real, and packed with the practical steps you need to move from surviving to thriving.

Part III: (Available December 2025) Freedom has GPS ~ Set Your Destination to Success

Each offering is a tool to help you rise, no matter where you're starting from. The journey to success isn't easy, but with the right tools, guidance, and mindset, you'll realize that every setback is just fuel for your comeback. Let's get to work, CEO.

I Humbly Thank You for your trust in the process!!

Made in the USA
Monee, IL
19 May 2025

17638478R00049